Once Upon A Tradition

**Using Traditional Literature
To Develop
Reading, Writing, Thinking,
and Research Skills**

The Giant

written and illustrated
by
Jan Grubb Philpot

Incentive Publications, Inc.
Nashville, Tennessee

Cover and illustrations by Jan Grubb Philpot
Edited by Jan Keeling

ISBN 0-86530-286-3

PRINTED IN THE UNITED STATES OF AMERICA

Table of Contents

"Old Mother Goose, when she wanted to wander, would ride through the air on a very fine gander!"

There is no dispute among educators in regard to the value of traditional literature in the classroom. Beyond being just good satisfying stories that spark imagination in our students, folktales hold a rightful place in our literary and cultural heritage. They lay the foundation for understanding all literature to follow. Many allusions in more modern fiction, poetry, and drama are simply not understandable without knowing the myths, fables, and folktales from whence they come. Further, many of our words, phrases, and figures of speech directly spring from folklore.

At one time in our society we could safely say that a good many of our children knew their Mother Goose and most familiar folktales. However, as a children's librarian, former secondary grades librarian, and an instructor of university children's literature classes, I feel qualified to say that can no longer be assumed. The days of video games, television, and mass media have begun to rob us of the treasures children once learned at mother's knee. How sad!

This book is designed to give teachers a basis for instilling in children a love and appreciation not only for the stories themselves but for the qualities of those stories that made them so beloved by countless generations.

Enjoy!

WELCOME

LET'S get acquainted!

The activities in this section will refamiliarize students with major folktales, and are intended to "hook 'em" on reading!

HAVE YOU HUGGED A WITCH TODAY?

⇨Check out the Folktales!

𝒯his activity will have students delving into the plots of traditional stories (some of which they may not have yet discovered!) for answers to "title" clues. This can be an individual or a group activity.

HERE'S HOW:

1. Reproduce the "books" on pages 10–12. Enlarge on colored paper or posterboard using an opaque projector or a duplicating machine. (You may choose to color the books with light colored markers.) Display books in a learning center or on a bulletin board.

2. Make a copy of the answer sheet on page 9 for each individual or team.

3. Explain to students that the Enchanted Kingdom Public Library has "titles" in which every character in the kingdom will be interested! Students are to match the "titles" in the display with the appropriate characters on their worksheets. This may be treated as a spare-time activity or as a creative homework assignment.

4. Give every team or individual completing the worksheet a "Key to the Kingdom" award (page 13).

FOLLOW-UP/VARIATION:

Stretch students' imaginations! Have each student make a list of ten to fifteen traditional story characters and create original titles to match!

Answer Key (to page 9)
> The Frog Prince — "A Princely Beginning"
> Cinderella — "From Rags to Riches"
> Little Red Riding Hood — "What a Wolf Looks Like"
> Maid in *Rumpelstiltskin* — "Encyclopedia of Unusual Names"
> Miss Muffet — "Spiders and How To Avoid Them"
> Henny Penny — "What To Do When the Sky Falls"
> Sluefoot Sue — "The Life Story of Pecos Bill"
> Three Billy Goats Gruff — "The Grass Is Greener on the Other Side"
> Rumpelstiltskin — "Straw to Gold in 12 Easy Steps"
> Sleeping Beauty — "Understanding Your Dream Life"
> Anansi — "Spider Teamwork"
> Paul Bunyan — "Lumbering Made Easy"
> Davy Crockett — "How To Tame and Ride a Bear"
> Strega Nona — "100 Ways To Fix Pasta!"
> Brer Rabbit — "A Rabbit's Comprehensive Guide to the Briar Patch"

It's been a busy day in the *Enchanted Kingdom's Public Library* ... it seems that a lot of characters have been in to "check things out"! The library has something for *everyone* — Examine titles in the display and match them to the character below that is most likely to be interested!

The Frog Prince _____

Cinderella _____

Little Red Riding Hood _____

Maid in *Rumpelstiltskin* _____

Miss Muffet _____

Henny Penny _____

Sluefoot Sue _____

Three Billy Goats Gruff _____

Rumpelstiltskin _____

Sleeping Beauty _____

Anansi _____

Paul Bunyan _____

Davy Crockett _____

Strega Nona _____

Brer Rabbit _____

100 ways to fix PASTA!
by Pasta Experience

LUMBERING MADE EASY
by Ina Woods

Spiders and How to Avoid Them
by I. Bite

From Rags to Riches
by I. M. Godmother

The Grass is greener on the Other Side
by Crossa Bridge

10

Straw to Gold in 12 Easy Steps
by Rich Mann

WHAT TO DO WHEN THE SKY FALLS
by Outta Blue

A Rabbit's Comprehensive Guide to the Briar Patch
by I. R. Hurt

What a Wolf Looks Like
by R. U. Fooled

Spider Teamwork
by Ina Webb

The Life Story of Pecos Bill
by Bill T. A. Haus

Encyclopedia of Unusual Names
by Gzrofngz

A Princely Beginning
by Ken B. Hoppin

How to Tame and Ride a BEAR
by E.Z. Fall

Understanding Your Dream Life
by Sheza Nappin

You deserve the

Key to the Kingdom

AWARD

for "checking out" the folktales in the library!

Congratulations, _____!

Teacher _____

Date _____

Helping Wishes Come True!

This is another activity intended to involve students in folklore and expose them to stories they should know, but may be unfamiliar with.

1. Duplicate the items on pages 16–19. You may choose to enlarge them using an opaque projector or a duplicating machine and color them (or duplicate on colored paper). Display them along with the "Fairy Godmother's Shopping List" (page 20) in a learning center or on a bulletin board.

2. For best results, pull from the library copies of the folktales involved and display them with the items. Note: Although specific characters are intended for each item, understand that creative thinkers well-versed in folklore may have perfectly logical alternative answers!

3. Reproduce enough worksheets (page 21) for individual students or teams participating in the activity.

4. Give each individual or team completing the activity an award (page 15).

Answer Key
1. The Hare ("The Tortoise and the Hare")
2. Three Soldiers ("Stone Soup")
3. Snow White
4. The Boy in "Soap, Soap, Soap" ("Grandfather Tale")
5. Brer Rabbit ("Uncle Remus" stories)
6. The Gingerbread Boy
7. The Beast ("Beauty and the Beast")
8. Little Red Riding Hood
9. Baby Bear ("The Three Bears")
10. Pecos Bill

11. The Three Little Pigs
12. Rapunzel
13. Hansel and Gretel
14. The Three Billy Goats Gruff
15. Rose ("The Talking Eggs")
16. The Little Red Hen
17. King Midas
18. The Grasshopper ("The Ant and the Grasshopper")
19. Iguana ("Why Mosquitoes Buzz in People's Ears")
20. Mrs. Peter Pumpkin-Eater (of "Mother Goose")

Note: If these stories are not all available to you, choose only items matching the titles you were able to find, and match your numbers on the worksheets accordingly. "White out" those characters for which you do not have items or books on "Fairy Godmother's Shopping List."

THANKS FOR *Helping Wishes Come True*

FOR CHARACTERS IN THE KINGDOM!

YOU DID AN ENCHANTING JOB!

DATE _____   TEACHER _____

1.

2.
Vegetable Soup

3.
Poisoned Apple Neutralizer

4.
SOAP

5.
Tar Solvent

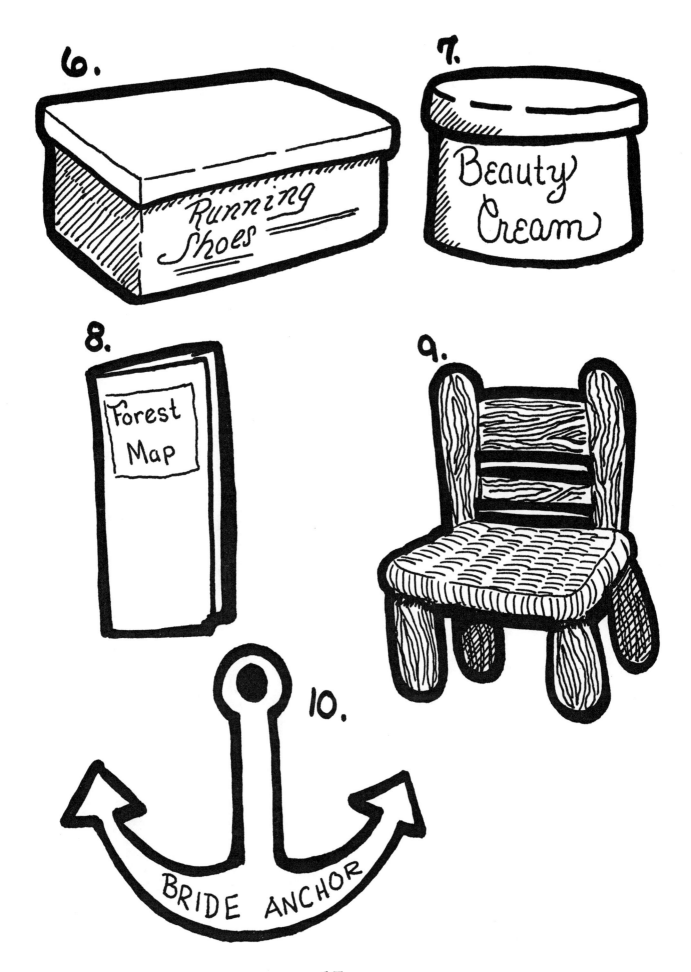

6. Running Shoes

7. Beauty Cream

8. Forest Map

9.

10. BRIDE ANCHOR

11.

WOLF
REPELLENT

12.

COUPON
Good For A
one-year supply
of hair conditioner

13.

SAFE
SWEETS

14.

TROLL
Detector

15.

BAD EGG FINDER

16.

one-year supply of HOMEMADE BREAD

17.

GREED
will get you
Nowhere

18.

JOB LISTINGS
your guide to immediate Employment!

19.

20.

PUMPKIN SHELL CRACKER

from the desk
of
Fairy Godmother

Be sure to shop for:

Brer Rabbit
Little Red Hen
The Grasshopper
King Midas
Iguana
Snow White
3 Soldiers
Pecos Bill
Baby Bear
The Beast
  3 Billy Goats Gruff
  3 Pigs

Gingerbread Boy
Hansel and Gretel
Little Red Riding Hood
Rapunzel
The Hare
Boy on "Grandfather
      Tale Lane"
Rose of "Talking
     Eggs" Forest
Mrs. Peter
    Pumpkin-Eater

The *Fairy Godmother* was determined to make wishes come true for folktale characters. She made a shopping list and went on a spree at Magic Mall — but when she returned to the Kingdom, she couldn't remember the character each item was intended for! *Can You help her?* Examine the items in the display. Match the number of the item to the line below, and fill in the name of the character who would most appreciate the gift.

1. _____

2. _____

3. _____

4. _____

5. _____

6. _____

7. _____

8. _____

9. _____

10. _____

11. _____

12. _____

13. _____

14. _____

15. _____

16. _____

17. _____

18. _____

19. _____

20. _____

THE NATURE OF THE BEAST!

Folktales differ from other types of literature. They have unique characteristics in their setting, plot, characterization, style, and theme. This may be because they spring from the oral storytelling tradition.

The activities in this section will help children understand the elements of traditional literature in an enjoyable way. At the same time, they will be exposed to a bit more of their cultural heritage in literature, something that is all too often forgotten in this age of multimedia and busy lifestyles.

Beginnings... and Endings

A folktale's setting is not introduced by long, descriptive passages. A simple phrase, "once upon a time," invites the listener to a magical place where anything can happen. Typical of folklore, too, is a formulaic ending that provides a satisfying conclusion to the plot.

• Reproduce the form at the bottom of this page. Have students examine a number of copies of written folktales in the library—they are found in the 398 section (nonfiction) of the library—and compare opening and closing phrases!

And/or

• Reproduce the "Beginnings" worksheet on page 24 and the "Endings" worksheet on page 25. Acquaint students with oft-used phrases in the introductions and conclusions of folktales. Then invite them to create their own!

FOLKTALE	OPENING	CLOSING

Beginnings

The setting of a folktale is not long or descriptive. A simple phrase tells the listener that he or she is in a place and time that is magical . . . anything can happen!

- Once upon a time . . .
- Long, long ago . . .
- Once there was, and twice there wasn't . . .
- In a faraway place, in a faraway time . . .
- Once long ago . . . so long I've forgotten how long ago it was . . .
- In the beginning . . .
- So long ago I was not there . . . or I would not be here to tell the tale . . .

MAKE UP YOUR OWN FOLKTALE BEGINNINGS BELOW:

_____

_____

_____

_____

_____

_____

_____

_____

And Endings

A one- or two-line "formula" ending frequently signals the conclusion of a folktale. Read the following typical endings found in folktales, and then create some of your own.

- And they lived happily ever after.
- My tale is done, away it has run.
- Snip, snap, snout. This tale's run out.
- And as far as I know, they live happily still.
- The tale has run to its end. Lock up the rooster, let out the hen.
- I was there and would be there still, if I hadn't come to tell the tale.

MAKE UP YOUR OWN FOLKTALE ENDINGS BELOW:

_____

_____

_____

_____

_____

_____

_____

_____

_____

WHICH WITCH IS WHICH?

One characteristic of traditional literature is the frequent use of common characters. For example, trolls are frequently found in Scandinavian folklore, fairies in French folklore, and giants in British folklore. One character that seems to cross many geographical boundaries is the witch. The witch has managed to escape the confines of traditional literature and maintain her status as a villain in classics, modern fiction, and poetry.

This fun-filled activity will acquaint children with common characters in traditional literature and the borrowing of those same characters for more recent fiction.

WHICH WITCH IS WHICH?

1. Reproduce ten copies of the "witch" on page 28. On the placard each witch holds, write one of the clues listed on the following page. Display your "woggle of witches" (apologies to Adrienne Adams) in a learning center or on a bulletin board. You may also choose to display the books involved. (Note: Be sure to number the witches!)

2. Explain the concept of common characters to the students. Brainstorm and list folk and fairy tales in which princesses, fairy godmothers, wolves, and other characters appear.

3. Give each student a "Which Witch Is Which?" worksheet (top of page 29) and challenge each to read the clues and identify the story associated with each witch. The students may examine books in your display if necessary. This may be done as an individual or group activity.

4. Give each student or team identifying all "witches" an award (page 29, bottom).

"WHICH WITCH IS WHICH?"

CLUES

1. Do you like pasta steaming hot?
   You'll have to see my magic pot!

2. Hungry and want something good to eat?
   Visit my house! It's really sweet!

3. I may be a witch, but I got a good scare
   When I spied a house flying through the air!

4. Are you sure I'm a witch? I might not be!
   But you'll have to read a book to see!

5. Princes that make me hopping mad
   Are liable to hop themselves—too bad!

6. If you're restless and can't seem to go to sleep . . .
   I've just the cure—a hundred years deep!

7. Which witch am I? Well, here's the clue:
   I've got a poisoned apple just for you!

8. Push clothes aside and walk through the door.
   I live in Narnia with magic galore!

9. Princes are in for a very bad scare
   When they seek ladies with long golden hair.

10. My house is high up in the air.
    Chicken legs hold it up and take me everywhere!

ANSWERS

1. Strega Nona (from the Italian folktale retold by Tomie dePaola)
2. The witch in "Hansel and Gretel"
3. The witch in *The Wizard of Oz* by Frank Baum
4. The witch in Lorna Balian's *Humbug Witch*
5. The witch in "The Frog Prince"
6. The witch in "Sleeping Beauty"
7. The witch in "Snow White"
8. The witch in *The Lion, the Witch, and the Wardrobe* by C. S. Lewis
9. The witch in "Rapunzel"
10. The witch in "Baba Yaga"

WHICH WITCH IS WHICH?

Kids! Each of the displayed witches have a role in folklore or modern fiction. They look the same... but they're not ... WHICH WITCH IS WHICH? Write the title below.

1. _____
2. _____
3. _____
4. _____
5. _____
6. _____
7. _____
8. _____
9. _____
10. _____

YOU SWEPT UP THIS AWARD by figuring out **WHICH WITCH WAS WHICH!** Congratulations!

Teacher _____

Date _____

Heroes and Villains

olktale characters are usually described as "flat," meaning their personalities do not change during the course of the story. Folktale characters are symbolic of either good or evil. For example, traditional witches are always "very, very bad" and the reader expects them to be. Fairy godmothers are always "very, very good," kind, and loving. This activity revolves around recognition of this particular aspect of folktales.

HEROES AND VILLAINS

- After exposing your students to a good many folktales, introduce the concept of "flat" characterization. Brainstorm to come up with a list of typical "evil" characters and a list of typical "good" characters.

- Reproduce the "Wanted in the Kingdom" poster on page 31 and the "Reward Worthy of a King's Ransom" poster on page 32. Allow each student to choose either a folktale hero or villain from the list of good and evil characters and creatively illustrate and describe the character on one of the posters. This activity can serve as an alternative form of book reporting.

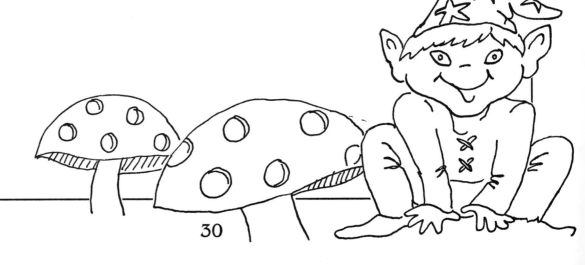

WANTED
in the kingdom

Name/Alias: _____

General description: _____

_____

Story affiliation: _____

Last known whereabouts: _____

Crime: _____

_____

A REWARD
worthy of a king's ransom

To _____

HEAR YE! HEAR YE! To all readers of the kingdom, let it be known that the above-named of the folktale _____ deserves a reward for performance of the following good deed:

_____
_____
_____
_____
_____

ON THE TRAIL OF FOLKTALES

WITCHES	KINGS	PRINCESSES	PRINCES
Snow White Baba Yaga Hansel and Gretel Rapunzel	King Cole Chicken Little	Sleeping Beauty The Princess and the Pea 12 Dancing Princesses	Snow White Sleeping Beauty The Frog Prince

On the Trail of Folktales is an activity that will inspire students to explore traditional literature and help them discover that certain motifs (or elements) in plot appear and reappear in this genre. At the same time, I'm sure you'll "catch 'em reading"!

Some of the most common plot motifs occurring in traditional literature are:

- **characters:** wolves, witches, giants, godmothers, fairies, princesses, trolls
- **magic objects:** a magic cooking pot, lamp, cloth, cloak
- **magic spells or powers:** invisibility, a long sleep, ability to fly, a magic transformation
- **others:** use of the number 3 (3 wishes, 3 attempts to do something, 3 main characters), trickery utilized by the main character

PLANNING SUGGESTIONS

1. Read several folk and fairy tales aloud to the class. Bring student attention to the fact that the same elements are used again and again in traditional literature. Once you make them consciously aware of this fact, it will be no trouble for them to brainstorm with you and list all the stories they can think of that use one of the elements listed on page 33.

2. Make a bulletin board or chart listing the various motifs for which you would like for the class to look and leaving space underneath to list the various stories in which these motifs appear. You may choose to enlarge some of the many folktale characters that appear as illustrations in this book to brighten up your bulletin board or chart.

3. Divide the class into teams and give each team captain a worksheet (page 35) on which motifs will be listed. Point teams in the direction of the 398 section of the library where traditional literature is found. (Note: You may also wish the students to use "contemporary" folktales/fairy tales, that is, those not passed down in the oral tradition and which have an attributable author. In this case, they should be sure not to miss the work of Hans Christian Andersen, usually found in the fiction section of the library.

   Students should be instructed to list all the stories they can find in which a particular element is found. For example, for princes they might list "The Frog Prince," "Sleeping Beauty," and "Snow White." It is natural for students to gravitate toward the most familiar traditional literature in English-speaking countries, most of which tends to be British, German, or French. However, encourage students to explore all of the traditional literature on the shelves, and you will find them discovering unusual stories and elements: spiders from Africa and trolls from Scandinavia!

   Give each student a bookmark (bottom of page 36) on which to keep track of unusual tales or of stories they might want to read later! If you want to make this a team contest, give each team a different colored marker to fill in their "finds" on the chart or bulletin board, and give an award (top of page 36) to the team finding the most examples.

4. As a follow-up activity, have students write their own folktales or fairy tales using several of the motifs they have discovered. Use the writing activity, "Cooperative Fairy Tales," page 45, if you wish to make this a group project. Be sure to assign each student one of the lesser-known folktales to read and share with the class.

The Wolf

On the trail of Folktales

ELEMENTS (motifs)	STORY EXAMPLES

Other common elements discovered

Congratulations!
You discovered many **Secrets** of the kingdom & are hereby entitled to this Award!

DATE _____   TEACHER _____

an award for great folktale "trackers"!

HAVE STUDENTS KEEP TRACK OF LESSER-KNOWN TALES THEY COME ACROSS.

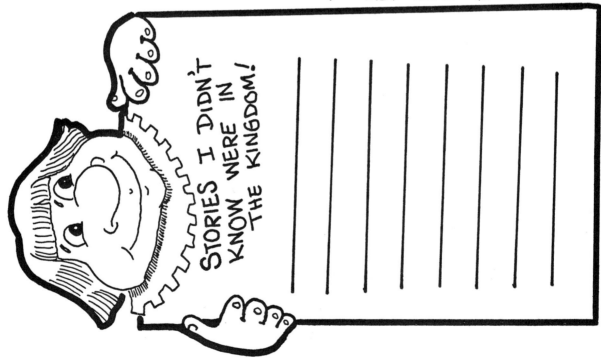

STORIES I DIDN'T KNOW WERE IN THE KINGDOM!

WHO said that?

The style in which folktales and fairy tales are written has its own peculiar characteristics. One of the most obvious characteristics is the use of rhymes, verses, and repetitive phrases. In fact, this is one of the reasons folktales and fairy tales appeal to young children.

This activity will refamiliarize students with beloved folktales, introduce them to some they may never have been exposed to, and make them aware of the written style of traditional literature.

HERE'S HOW:

1. Reproduce and cut out the dialogue "balloons" on pages 38–42. You may choose to enlarge them using an opaque projector or a copy machine. Post the "balloons" (without the speaking character!) in a learning center or on a bulletin board.

2. Obtain copies of the appropriate folktales from the media center and place near your display.

3. Instruct students to number answer sheets one through twenty, examine the selections in the display, and determine "Who Said That?" for each quotation. They should write both the character and the name of the folktales or fairy tale used. This can be an individual or team spare-time activity.

4. When all the quotations have been attributed to a character, have each student draw one of the characters. Post the illustrations beneath the appropriate dialogue "balloon."

ANSWERS

1. "The Gingerbread Boy" or the "Pancake Man"
2. The witch, "Hansel and Gretel"
3. The frog, "The Frog Prince"
4. The troll, "The Three Billy Goats Gruff"
5. The giant, "Jack and the Beanstalk"
6. Any of the three pigs, "The Three Little Pigs"
7. The wicked queen/stepmother, "Snow White"
8. "Red Riding Hood"
9. "The Little Red Hen"
10. The prince, "Rapunzel"
11. Any of the three bears, "The Three Bears"
12. "Henny Penny"
13. The wolf, "The Three Little Pigs"
14. The bridge, "The Three Billy Goats Gruff"
15. "Rumpelstiltskin"
16. The wolf, "The Three Little Pigs"
17. The old woman, "The Old Woman and Her Pig"
18. The giant, "Jack and the Beanstalk"
19. "The Boy Who Cried Wolf"
20. The three French soldiers, "Stone Soup"

Across the World
variants of familiar tales

It is fascinating to learn that variations of the same folktales crop up again and again throughout the world. Perhaps the characters in one tale are slightly different from those in another, or are called by different names, but the same basic plot is recognizable to the listener.

For example, "Cinderella" (from France) is "Tattercoats" in England, "Ashenputtel" in Germany, and "Yeh-Shen" in China. In the French version, Cinderella is visited by a fairy godmother, in the English version she is aided by a gooseherd, and in the German version her gifts come from a bird. It is interesting that the Vietnamese Cinderella (Tarn) receives her gifts from the bones of a much-loved fish!

In recent years, many variants of the old familiar tales have been adapted and published for children. You are given a list of some of these on page 44.

Help students realize the cultural ties that bind our world, expose them to more folklore, and make them aware of cultural differences with the following activity.

Divide students into groups and give them each several copies of variants of the same folktale. Have them examine these variants and create a comparison chart. Some of the characteristics that might be compared are: name, setting, characters, spells, problems, solutions, opening and closing phrases, chants or refrains, and any characteristic relating to the particular story being compared.

CHART EXAMPLE:

Characteristic being compared	Cinderella	Ashenputtel	Tattercoats

Folktales across the World

This list of folktale variants is by no means complete, but simply intended as an aid to you.

CINDERELLA

The Brocaded Slipper (Vietnam). Lynette Dyer Vuong. Addison-Wesley, 1982.

Cinderella (France). Feni Montresor. Knopf, 1965.

Cinderella (France). Charles Perrault. Scribner, 1954.

Tattercoats (English). Flora A. Steel. Bradbury, 1976.

Yeh-Shen (China). Ai-Lang Louie. Philomel, 1982.

THE GINGERBREAD BOY

"The Bun" (Russia). James Riordan. *Tales from Central Russia*, Kestrel Books, 1979.

The Gingerbread Boy (England). Paul Galdone. Clarion Books, 1975.

Journey Cake, Ho! (America/Appalachia). Ruth Sawyer. Viking, 1953.

JACK AND THE BEANSTALK

Jack and the Beanstalk (England). Lorinda B. Cauley. Putnam, 1983.

Jack and the Wonder Beans (America/Appalachia). James Still. Putnam, 1977.

RAPUNZEL

Petrosinella (Italy). Giambattista Basile. Warne, 1981.

Rapunzel (Germany). Bernadette Watts. Crowell, 1975.

RUMPELSTILTSKIN

Duffy and the Devil (England, recent retelling). Harve Zemach. Farrar, Straus, 1973.

Rumpelstiltskin (Germany). Donna Diamond. Holiday, 1983.

"The Talking Fish" (Armenia). Virginia Tashjian. *Once There Was and Was Not, Armenian Tales Retold*. Little, Brown, 1971.

Tom Tit Tot (England). Evaline Ness. Scribner, 1965.

"Whippety Stourie" (Scotland). Barbara Ker Wilson. *Scottish Folk-tales and Legends*, Walck, 1954.

SLEEPING BEAUTY

"Little Briar-Rose" (Germany). Jakob Grimm. *The Complete Grimm's Fairy Tales*, Pantheon, 1974.

"Sleeping Beauty" (France). Charles Perrault. *Perrault's Complete Fairy Tales*, Dodd, Mead, 1982.

STONE SOUP

"Hatchet Gruel" (Russia). Mirra Ginsburg. *Three Rolls and One Doughnut: Fables from Russia*, Dial, 1970.

Nail Soup (Sweden). Adapted from text by Nils Djurklo. Follett, 1964.

Stone Soup (France). Marcia Brown. Scribner, 1947.

THE MAGIC PORRIDGE POT

"The Enormous Genie" (Armenia). Virginia Tashjian. *Three Apples Fell from Heaven, Armenian Tales Retold*, Little, Brown, 1971.

The Funny Little Woman (Japan). Arlene Mosel. Dutton, 1972.

"Jack and the North West Wind" (America/Appalachia). Richard Chase. *The Jack Tales*, Houghton Mifflin, 1943.

"The Lad Who Went to the North Wind" (Norway). Peter Asbjornsen and Jorgen E. Moe. *East O' the Sun and West O' the Moon*, Dover, 1970.

The Magic Porridge Pot (Germany). Paul Galdone. Seabury, 1976.

The Magic Cooking Pot (India). Faith M. Towle. Houghton Mifflin, 1975.

The Table, the Donkey, and the Stick (Germany). Paul Galdone. McGraw-Hill, 1976.

Cooperative Fairy Tales
a group writing experience

Cooperative fairy tales use traditional tales as springboards for a great writing experience. Here's how:

1. A simple way to begin is to read aloud Jon Scieszka's *The Frog Prince, Continued* (Viking). Because this is (obviously) a creative continuation of the old familiar tale, it is a great way to introduce the concept of writing extensions to the "happily ever after" endings of any folktale. In *The Frog Prince, Continued*, the prince decides he is unhappy with his new situation and wishes once again to become a frog. He searches for help and in the process runs into witches from *Hansel and Gretel*, *Snow White*, *Sleeping Beauty*, not to mention the fairy godmother of *Cinderella*. This plot structure makes it ideal for . .

2. . . . introducing the concept of common motifs appearing in folktales! (Of course, if you have already used the activity "On the Trail of Folktales," page 33, you are one step ahead of the game!)

3. List common motifs or occurrences in fairy tales on the board, such as Good Characters, Bad Characters, Spells, How Spells Are Cast, How Spells Are Broken, Setting, and Powers. Have students brainstorm for ideas they remember from various fairy tales.

4. Explain to the class members that they will be writing an original fairy tale together. Divide the class into teams and appoint a captain of each. Have one team decide on one or two "good characters" for the story. Have another team decide on one or two "bad characters" for the story. Still another team can decide where the story takes place: in a castle? a cottage? a condominium? Where else could it be? Yet another team decides what is going to happen to one of the main characters: a disappearance? a transformation? a deep sleep? a kidnapping?

Allow the teams time to whisper among themselves. As they decide, have the team captains raise their hands to report to you. Write their decisions on the board and instruct them to sit quietly until each team has reported back to you.

5. Tell the story to the class as you now know it. For example, what you now know might go something like this:

"Once upon a time there was a prince, a princess, and a witch who lived in a castle. One day the prince disappeared."

Obviously, this is not yet a story, but it certainly has the makings of one! Now, throw back the unanswered questions to the class:

"Who made the prince disappear?" "Why was the prince made to disappear?" "Did the prince just disappear or did he turn into something?" Give each unanswered question to a team and repeat the process. Now you might get something like this:

"Once upon a time, there was a prince and a princess who lived in a castle. A witch who lived nearby was jealous, so she decided to get rid of the prince. She turned him into a turkey sandwich."

6. This brings up fresh questions! Just repeat the process, each time reviewing the story as you know it before bringing up new questions. You will be surprised how soon it will turn into a very creative fairy tale. In fact, this one did! See page 48 for "Beauty and the Sandwich" by a real first grade class.

Caution: While you are encouraging students to think further with their answers and prodding them at times to be more creative with their solutions (who says it has to be a poisoned apple? What's wrong with a hot dog?), avoid feeding students your own ideas. They are quite capable of being more imaginative than we adults are!

7. Once the process is finished, have a class "scribe" write down the story, or better yet, have everyone write his or her version. Then assign characters and events from the story to everyone in the class to illustrate.

8. "Publish" a class picture book of the story. Trim the illustrations the students have drawn and pull selected sentences from their writing to use as text. Do "paste ups" and bind the pages. Be sure to include illustrations and/or manuscript from each member of the class. Let the entire class sign the title page of the book.

Following are three stories done just this way by very real primary classrooms. Each story made adorable six- to eight-page books to which every member of the class contributed. I was as proud of these books as were the students, and it was quite difficult deciding just which ones to share with you! Hope you like them!

This activity tends to aid even the most ambivalent writer in gaining the confidence to write. There is a definite structure underlying traditional tales. With your questions, you have modeled the revision steps in writing. Challenge students now to branch out and write an original tale of their own!

Beauty and the Sandwich
by a 1st grade class

Once upon a time there was a prince and a princess who lived in a castle and were very happy! There were so happy they made an old witch who lived nearby very angry! The witch decided she would put a spell on the prince. She would turn him into a . . . turkey sandwich! He would get eaten up and be gone. So she did that. When the princess passed the turkey sandwich lying on a plate, she remembered she was hungry! When her lips touched the sandwich . . . he turned back into a prince!! The witch was so angry, she got hotter and hotter . . . until she melted! The prince and the princess lived happily ever after!

The Princess and the Beast
by a 2nd grade class

Once upon a time there was a prince, a princess, and a fairy godmother who lived together in a castle. They were very happy. But not far away lived a very ugly beast who was very unhappy! He was jealous of the happiness of the prince and princess and wished he had a beast wife. So he kidnapped the princess, waved a magic wand, said "hocus pocus" and "abracadabra" and she was instantly turned into a beast! The prince was heartbroken! He ran to the fairy godmother and asked her what to do. She told him to break the spell he must kiss the beast, so he ran to the beast's house, kissed his once-princess-now-beast, and she instantly turned back into a princess! They went home and lived happily ever after, and the beast went to (name of a well-know discount chain) because you can find anything there, got a beast wife, and was happy ever after!

pizza

The King's Rescue of the Fairy Godmother
by a 1st grade class

Spell book

Once there was a king and a queen who lived in a castle with a fairy godmother who loved pizza and took care of them. Not far away lived an ugly dragon who wanted to be mean to the king and queen, but the fairy godmother wouldn't let him. So he decided to get rid of her. He sent to (well-known pizza chain) and ordered a pizza which he poisoned. Sure enough, when the pizza was delivered, the fairy godmother gobbled it right down and fell into a deep sleep . . . *zzzz*. When the king found her he was upset! Everyone knows a fairy godmother can break spells, but what was a king to do? So he went to the public library to find a book about spells. At last he knew just what to do! He came home, gave the fairy godmother a kiss and a hug. She woke up, and they all lived happily ever after.

The witch was so angry, she gotten hotter and hotter until she melted.

discover the world *in a folktale*

Send your students on a world tour—via folktales! Folktales abound in every culture. A bit of the flavor of the culture always seeps through in its folklore!

Motivate your students with the idea of reading their way around the world with traditional literature. Reproduce the "magic carpet" on page 51 for each member of the class. Reproduce the guide to "Folktales Around the World," pages 52–54, as well. You may ask your librarian to reserve for your class as many of these folktales as are available. Invite students to step aboard their "magic carpets" and fly away to parts unknown!

OPTIONAL IDEAS FOR A SUCCESSFUL PROGRAM:

• Display a world map during this program. Students will naturally want to know their location as they travel the globe. You might wish to attach appropriate story titles to various countries on the map. You may also choose to reproduce the world map (page 55). As students read a title indigenous to a country, they may research the country's boundaries and color in the country. If they use colored markers, they can "color-code" by filling in their title on the "magic carpet" in the same color.

• Design a reading corner complete with posters or photographs of sights throughout the world (ask a travel agency for donations of old posters or ask a "world traveler" to share photos). Put "magic carpets" (throw rugs) on the floor for students to lounge on as they read!

• As a student reads a folktale, have him or her write the title and country on the magic carpet. In lieu of a standard book report, a student can illustrate a "souvenir" from the country visited (for example, a tiny shoe from Germany's "The Shoemaker and the Elves") and explain beneath the illustration how the souvenir ties in with the story.

• Give each student an award (page 51) when he or she has "visited" a specified number of countries.

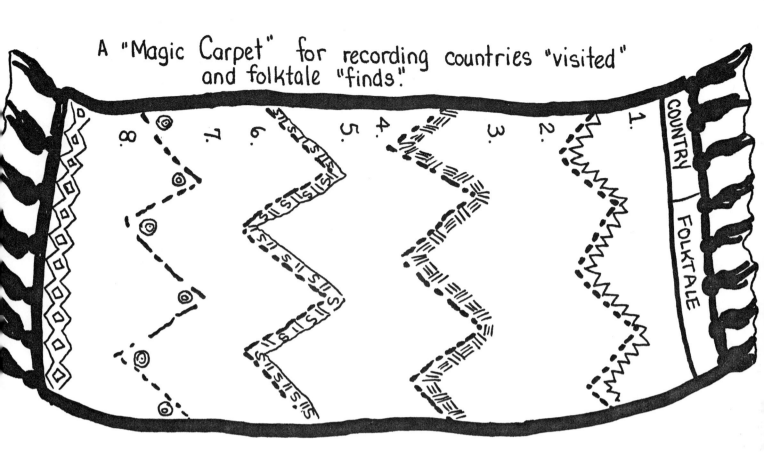

A "Magic Carpet" for recording countries "visited" and folktale "finds."

COUNTRY	FOLKTALE

so glad you discovered the world of folktales!

Congratulations,

_____, for "flying" right in there and getting it done!

Date _____   Teacher _____

51

Folktales across the world

a guide to folktales from various cultures

Two of the best sources of folktales from various cultures are found in anthologies by May Hill Arbuthnot:

The Arbuthnot Anthology of Children's Literature. Revised by Zena Sutherland. Scott, Foresman, and Co., 1976.

Time for Fairy Tales. Scott, Foresman, and Co., 1961.

In these books you will find folktales from the following cultures: Great Britain, Ireland, Germany, Scandinavia, Finland, Spain, Italy, Poland, Czechoslovakia, Russia, Turkey, Africa, China, Japan, Korea, Vietnam, India, Australia, Canada, United States of America, West Indies, and Latin America.

While these are wonderful collections, chances are you will want sources that are single editions as well, with plenty of delightful illustrations. The following list was devised in recognition of this need.

AFRICAN

Aardema, Verna. *Bringing the Rain to Kapiti Plain: A Nandi Tale.* Dial, 1981.

Ibid. *Why Mosquitoes Buzz in People's Ears: A West African Folk Tale.* Dial, 1975.

Haley, Gail. *A Story, a Story: An African Tale.* Atheneum, 1970.

McDermott, Gerald. *Anansi the Spider: A Tale from the Ashanti.* Holt, Rinehart, and Winston, 1972.

AMERICAN

African American

Bang, Molly. *Wiley and the Hairy Man.* Macmillan, 1976.

Hamilton, Virginia. *The People Could Fly.* Knopf, 1985.

Jaquith, Priscilla. *Bo Rabbit Smart for True: Folktales from the Gullah.* Philomel, 1981.

Keats, Ezra Jack. *John Henry: An American Legend.* Pantheon, 1965.

San Souci, Robert D. *The Talking Eggs.* Dial, 1989.

Appalachian

Chase, Richard. *Grandfather Tales.* Houghton Mifflin, 1948.

Ibid. *The Jack Tales.* Houghton Mifflin, 1943.

Still, James. *Jack and the Wonder Beans.* Putnam, 1977.

Native American

Baker, Betty. *Rat Is Dead and Ant Is Sad.* Harper and Row, 1981.

Baylor, Byrd. *And It Is Still That Way: Legends Told by Arizona Indian Children.* Scribner, 1976.

Goble, Paul. *The Gift of the Sacred Dog.* Bradbury, 1980.

Harris, Christie. *Once Upon a Totem.* Atheneum, 1973.

Highwater, Jamake. *Anpao: An American Indian Odyssey.* Lippincott, 1977.

McDermott, Gerald. *Arrow to the Sun: A Pueblo Indian Tale.* Viking, 1974.

BRITISH

Brown, Marcia. *Dick Whittington and His Cat.* Scribner, 1950.

Cauley, Lorinda B. *Goldilocks and the Three Bears.* Putnam, 1981.

De la Mare, Walter. *Mollie Whuppie.* Farrar, Straus, and Giroux, 1983.

Galdone, Paul. *The Little Red Hen.* Seabury, 1973.

Ibid. *The Three Bears.* Seabury, 1972.

Ibid. *The Three Sillies.* Houghton Mifflin, 1981.

Steele, Flora Annie. *Tattercoats.* Bradbury, 1976.

Zemach, Harve. *Duffy and the Devil.* Farrar, Straus, and Giroux, 1973.

CANADIAN

Barbeau, Marius. *The Golden Phoenix and Other French-Canadian Fairy Tales.* Walck, 1958.

Carlson, Natalie Savage. *The Talking Cat and Other Stories of French Canada.* Harper, 1952.

CHINESE

Louie, Ai-Lang. *Yeh-Shen: A Cinderella Story from China.* Philomel, 1982.

Mosel, Arlene. *Tikki Tikki Tembo.* Holt, 1968.

Richie, Alice. *The Treasure of Li-Po.* Harcourt, 1949.

Wolkstein, Diane. *White Wave: A Chinese Tale.* Crowell, 1979.

FRENCH

Berson, Harold. *The Thief Who Hugged a Moonbeam.* Seabury, 1972.

Ibid. *Balarin's Goat.* Crown, 1972.

Brown, Marcia. *Stone Soup.* Scribner, 1947.

De Beaumont, Madame. *Beauty and the Beast.* Bradbury, 1978.

Galdone, Paul. *Cinderella.* McGraw-Hill, 1978.

Ibid. *Puss in Boots.* Seabury, 1976.

Perrault, Charles. *The Sleeping Beauty.* Translated by David Walker. Crowell, 1976.

GERMAN

DeRegniers, Beatrice S. *Red Riding Hood.* Atheneum, 1972.

Galdone, Paul. *Hansel and Gretel.* McGraw-Hill, 1982.

Grimm, Jakob and Wilhelm. *The Shoemaker and the Elves.* Scribner, 1960.

Ibid. *The Sleeping Beauty.* Little, Brown, and Co., 1977.

Ibid. *Snow White and the Seven Dwarfs.* Farrar, Straus, and Giroux 1972.

Ibid. *The Traveling Musicians*. Harcourt, 1955.

Ibid. *Twelve Dancing Princesses*. Viking, 1978.

HISPANIC

Aardema Verna. *The Riddle of the Drum: A Tale from Tizapan, Mexico*. Four Winds Press, 1979.

DePaola, Tomie. *The Lady of Guadalupe*. Holiday, 1980.

ITALIAN

Basile, Giambattista. *Petrosinella*. Warne, 1981.

Chafetz, Henry. *The Legend of Befana*. Houghton Mifflin, 1958.

DePaola, Tomie. *Strega Nona: An Old Tale Retold*. Prentice Hall, 1975.

Haviland, Virginia. *Favorite Fairy Tales Told in Italy*. Little, Brown, and Co., 1967.

JAPANESE

Laurin, Anne. *The Perfect Crane*. Harper and Row, 1981.

McDermott, Gerald. *The Stonecutter: A Japanese Folk Tale*. Viking, 1975.

Mosel, Arlene. *The Funny Little Woman*. Dutton, 1972.

Pratt, Davis and Elsa Kula. *Magic Animals of Japan*. Parnassus, 1967.

JEWISH

McDermott, Beverly. *The Golem*. Lippincott, 1976.

Singer, Isaac Bashevis. *Mazel and Shlimazel, or the Milk of the Lioness*. Farrar, Straus, and Giroux, 1967.

Zemach, Margot. *It Could Always Be Worse*. Farrar, Straus, and Giroux, 1977.

NORWEGIAN

Asbjornsen, Peter C. and Jorgen E. Moe. *East of the Sun and West of the Moon and Other Tales*. MacMillan, 1963.

Ibid. *The Three Billy Goats Gruff*. Harcourt, Brace, Jovanovich, 1967.

D'Aulaire, Ingri and Edgar. *Trolls*. Doubleday, 1972.

Mayer, Mercer. *East of the Sun and West of the Moon*. Four Winds Press, 1980.

RUSSIAN

Afanasyev, Alexander. *Soldier and Tsar in the Forest: A Russian Tale*. Farrar, Straus, and Giroux, 1972.

Cole, Joanna. *Bony-Legs*. Four Winds Press, 1983.

Ginsburg, Mirra. *Three Rolls and One Doughnut*. Dial, 1970.

Harris, Rosemary. *The Flying Ship*. Faber and Faber, 1975.

Prokofieff, Serge. *Peter and the Wolf*. Knopf, 1940.

Tolstoy, Alexei. *The Great Big Enormous Turnip*. Watts, 1969.

Note: This bibliography is not a complete one. It is simply intended as an aid to you to begin your investigation of folktales around the world.

Discover the world of **Folktales!**

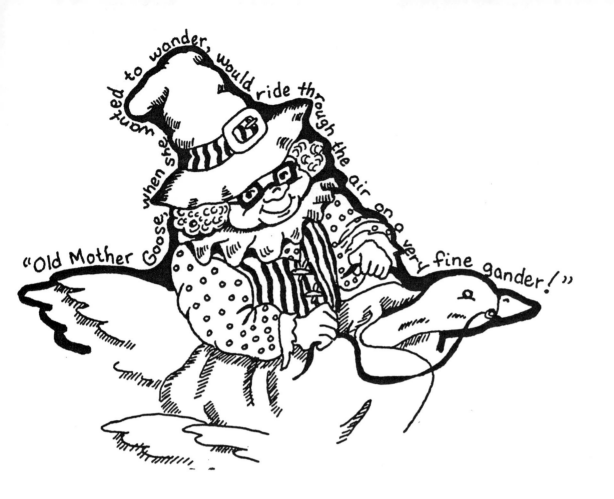

"Old Mother Goose, when she wanted to wander, would ride through the air on a very fine gander!"

Traditional Trivia

Knowing traditional literature: Mother Goose, Tall Tales, Fables, Mythology, Fairy Tales, & other folktales.

TRADITIONAL TRIVIA!

𝒯raditional trivia is a game children dearly love. It will expose them to tales in all major traditional literature categories, promote reading excitement, and, at the same time, keep interest and enthusiasm high!

HERE'S HOW:

Reproduce the question cards on pages 60–79. There are five categories:
Mother Goose
Tall Tales
Fables
Mythology
Fairy Tales and Other Folktales

To be especially well-organized, you may wish to reproduce the cards on papers of different colors (for example, Mother Goose—green; Fables—blue; Tall Tales—yellow; etc.). Clip the cards apart and laminate to ensure long-lasting usage.

RULES OF PLAY

There are obviously many ways the components of this game can be used, and I invite you to use your imagination! However, I would like to share with you the approach that I enjoy the most and which has been most effective for me when using the game as a whole-group activity.

1. Post the names of your categories where all can see them. You may limit the categories for younger students. For example, while first and second graders love this game, they are not yet ready for mythology. However, do not assume "Mother Goose" should be eliminated for 5th graders! They don't feel patronized a bit by having at least one category that is easy for the scoring of points.

Prince Charming

2. Divide the class into teams of five to six students. Appoint one student on each team as "captain." (Note: I like to appoint a different person on the team each time. I also like to be sure the first few times we play to appoint the least likely person as captain. I think it fun to watch the confidence of these students grow and their teammates' recognition of the importance of the role they play in the team's success.) Caution the other students on the team that they are not to speak aloud and that doing so will cause their team to lose a point. Team members are to converse with each other in whispers and agree on choices of categories and answers, but the captain has the final say and is the only team member allowed to communicate the team's answers. This not only fosters a spirit of teamwork and group cooperation, but immediately sets the pace for a controlled game rather than chaos. And—trust me—it does not dampen the interest and enthusiasm in the game one iota!

3. Explain to the students that each team will have its turn. The captain will tell you the chosen category, and you will ask the question. The team converses, and the captain relays the answer.

- If the answer is correct, the team gets a point and chooses another category. They continue in this manner until a question is answered incorrectly. (Note: They must answer one question from each category before they are allowed to return to the first category.)

- If a question is missed, play passes to the next team. (Note: This is very important. This is a learning game, even if it seems so much fun at times that the learning is forgotten. When a question is missed, repeat the question and tell the class the answer. Caution them that the question will come up again soon, and then slip the card two or three cards down from the top of the stack. It may take several instances of the same question being missed, but soon you will find students listening carefully!)

4. The game can stop at any point as long as each team has had the same number of turns. You can give awards or treats to the winners. If you choose (as I do) to make this an ongoing activity all year long, post an incentive chart and mark each team's win, with a treat given at the end of the year—or, if another teacher in your building does the same, have a contest at the end of the year between the top two teams! Either way, ask your librarian to stock up on traditional literature!

Mother Goose

Where was Simple Simon going when he met a pieman?

THE FAIR

Mother Goose

Who put the cat in the well?

LITTLE JOHNNY GREEN

Mother Goose

What did the old woman who lived in a shoe give her children to eat?

BROTH WITHOUT ANY BREAD

Mother Goose

Who jumped over a candlestick?

JACK

Mother Goose

What was Wee Willie Winkle wearing?

HIS NIGHTGOWN

Mother Goose

Who made tarts?

THE QUEEN OF HEARTS

Mother Goose

Who did the dish run away with?

THE SPOON

Mother Goose

Who went to the sea in a bowl?

THREE WISE MEN OF GOTHAM

Mother Goose

How many bags of wool did the black sheep have?

THREE

Mother Goose

Who pulled a plum from a pie?

LITTLE JACK HORNER

Mother Goose

What could Jack Spratt not eat?

FAT

Mother Goose

Who lost her pocket?

LUCY LOCKET

Mother Goose

Who stole a pig?

TOM, THE PIPER'S SON

Mother Goose

Who jumped over the moon?

THE COW

Mother Goose

Who ate curds and whey?

MISS MUFFET

Mother Goose

Who sang for his supper?

LITTLE TOMMY TUCKER

Mother Goose

What three things did King Cole call for?

HIS PIPE, HIS BOWL, HIS FIDDLERS THREE

Mother Goose

Who broke his crown?

JACK

Mother Goose

Who made the girls cry?

GEORGIE PORGIE

Mother Goose

Who fell asleep under a haystack?

LITTLE BOY BLUE

Mother Goose

What did the first little piggie do?

WENT TO THE MARKET

Mother Goose

Who were the three men in a tub?

THE BUTCHER, THE BAKER,
THE CANDLESTICK MAKER

Mother Goose

What grows in Mary's garden?

SILVER BELLS, COCKLE SHELLS,
AND PRETTY MAIDS ALL IN A ROW

Mother Goose

What did the farmer's wife do to
three mice?

CUT OFF THEIR TAILS

Tall Tales

What was the name of Davy Crockett's rifle?

BETSY

Tall Tales

What was the name of Mike Fink's rifle?

BANG-ALL

Tall Tales

Who was New York's biggest, bravest fireman?

MOSE

Tall Tales

What was the name of Pecos Bill's horse?

WIDOW MAKER

Tall Tales

Who bounced off the back of a wagon as a baby and wasn't missed?

PECOS BILL

Tall Tales

Who was the crafty farmer who tricked his neighbors into staying on the plains to farm?

FEBOLD FEBOLDSEN

Tall Tales

Who was raised by coyotes?

PECOS BILL

Tall Tales

Who was born with ocean water in his veins?

OLD STORMALONG

Tall Tales

Who was the steelworker that could stir molten iron with his bare arm?

JOE MAGARAC

Tall Tales

Who was know as the "steel-drivin' man"?

JOHN HENRY

Tall Tales

Who planted apple trees throughout the western United States?

JOHNNY APPLESEED

Tall Tales

Who made the white cliffs of Dover out of soap?

OLD STORMALONG

Tall Tales

Who tamed and rode a bear?

DAVY CROCKETT

Tall Tales

Who died with a hammer
in his hand?

JOHN HENRY

Tall Tales

What was the real name of
Johnny Appleseed?

JOHN CHAPMAN

Tall Tales

What was the name of Paul
Bunyan's pet ox?

BABE

Tall Tales

Who was the "bouncing bride"?

SLUEFOOT SUE

Tall Tales

Who was known as
"King of the River"?

MIKE FINK

Tall Tales

Who reached for a hammer instead of a rattle as a baby?

JOHN HENRY

Tall Tales

What two tall tale characters had a shooting contest?

MIKE FINK AND DAVY CROCKETT

Tall Tales

Who was the real-life railroad engineer who gave his life in a train crash to save passengers and crew?

CASEY JONES

Tall Tales

What tall tale hero could converse with the animals?

JOHNNY APPLESEED

Tall Tales

Who was the great "Bear-Hunter Preacher of the Magnolia State"?

MIKE HOOPER

Tall Tales

What color was Paul Bunyan's pet ox?

BLUE

Fables

Where did the dog decide to take his nap?

IN THE MANGER
("DOG IN THE MANGER")

Fables

What cousins decided to try out each other's homes?

COUNTRY MOUSE
AND CITY MOUSE

Fables

What did Androcles do for the lion?

PULLED A THORN FROM HIS PAW
("ANDROCLES AND THE LION")

Fables

How did the mouse repay the lion?

FREED HIM FROM
THE HUNTER'S NET
("THE MOUSE AND THE LION")

Fables

What did the fox work so hard for only to discover he didn't like them?

SOUR GRAPES
("THE FOX AND THE GRAPES")

Fables

What did the hare do that caused the tortoise to win the race?

TOOK A NAP
("THE HARE AND THE TORTOISE")

Fables

How did the crow reach the water in the jug?

PUT ROCKS IN THE JUG
("THE CROW IN THE PITCHER")

Fables

"Little friends may prove to be great friends" is the moral of what fable?

"THE LION AND THE MOUSE"

Fables

What was the ant willing to do that the grasshopper was not?

WORK; STORE FOOD FOR THE WINTER
("THE ANT AND THE GRASSHOPPER")

Fables

What kind of characters are most often found in fables?

ANIMALS

Fables

"United we stand, divided we fall" is the moral of what fable?

"THE OXEN AND THE LION"

Fables

What happened when the four oxen quarreled?

THE LION ATE THEM.
("THE OXEN AND THE LION")

Fables

Who took "the lion's share" of the hunt because he was biggest and strongest?

THE LION (OF COURSE!)

Fables

Why did the farmer kill the goose that laid the golden eggs?

HE HOPED TO FIND MORE GOLDEN EGGS INSIDE THE GOOSE. ("THE GOOSE THAT LAID GOLDEN EGGS")

Fables

What did the fox that lost his tail try to get his brothers to do?

CUT OFF THEIR TAILS, TOO ("THE FOX WITHOUT A TAIL")

Fables

Who learned there was no use offering a plan that could not be carried out?

THE MICE ("BELLING THE CAT")

Fables

Who learned to think twice before leaping?

THE FROGS

Fables

"It is best to think ahead and prepare for the lean times" is the moral of what fable?

"THE ANT AND THE GRASSHOPPER"

Fables

Who wanted to tie a bell around the cat's neck?

THE MICE ("BELLING THE CAT")

Fables

What did the shepherd boy do that made the villagers angry?

LIED ABOUT THE WOLF COMING ("THE BOY WHO CRIED WOLF")

Fables

What person do we associate with the telling of fables?

AESOP

Fables

"Slow and steady wins the race" is the moral of what fable?

"THE HARE AND THE TORTOISE"

Fables

From what fable do we get the saying, "It's just sour grapes"?

"THE FOX AND THE GRAPES"

Fables

What is the purpose of a fable?

TO TEACH A LESSON

Fairy Tales & Other Folktales

What young girl was locked in a tower?

RAPUNZEL

Fairy Tales & Other Folktales

Of what did the three pigs build their houses?

STRAW, STICKS, AND BRICK

Fairy Tales & Other Folktales

Who is the clever spider in African folktales?

ANANSI

Fairy Tales & Other Folktales

Who fooled Brer Fox and Brer Bear?

BRER RABBIT

Fairy Tales & Other Folktales

Who did all the work while her friends lazed away the day?

THE LITTLE RED HEN

Fairy Tales & Other Folktales

Who lived in the Russian woodlands in a house that stands on chicken legs?

BABA YAGA

Fairy Tales & Other Folktales

Who said, "My! What big ears you have!"?

LITTLE RED RIDING HOOD

Fairy Tales & Other Folktales

What two Chinese brothers fell into a well?

CHANG AND TIKKI TIKKI TEMBO

Fairy Tales & Other Folktales

What caused Sleeping Beauty to fall asleep?

SHE PRICKED HER FINGER ON A SPINDLE.

Fairy Tales & Other Folktales

What famous brothers collected the folktales of Germany?

THE GRIMM BROTHERS

Fairy Tales & Other Folktales

What did the wicked Oni make the funny little woman cook for them?

RICE DUMPLINGS

Fairy Tales & Other Folktales

Who ate the Gingerbread Boy?

THE FOX

Fairy Tales & Other Folktales

Who is famous for telling the Brer Rabbit stories?

UNCLE REMUS

Fairy Tales & Other Folktales

Who was sure the sky was falling?

CHICKEN LITTLE OR HENNY PENNY

Fairy Tales & Other Folktales

What did Goldilocks break?

BABY BEAR'S CHAIR

Fairy Tales & Other Folktales

What turned into a prince when kissed by a princess?

A FROG

Fairy Tales & Other Folktales

What did Jack trade for the beans that grew a beanstalk?

A COW

Fairy Tales & Other Folktales

Who ate a poisoned apple?

SNOW WHITE

Fairy Tales & Other Folktales

Who first shouted that the emperor was wearing no clothes?

A LITTLE BOY
("THE EMPEROR'S NEW CLOTHES")

Fairy Tales & Other Folktales

Who made shoes for the shoemaker?

THE ELVES
("THE ELVES AND THE SHOEMAKER")

Fairy Tales & Other Folktales

At what time did Cinderella's coach turn into a pumpkin?

MIDNIGHT

Fairy Tales & Other Folktales

Who guarded the bridge to the grassy hillside?

A TROLL
("THREE BILLY GOATS GRUFF")

Fairy Tales & Other Folktales

How did the princess prove she was real?

SHE FELT A PEA
UNDER A STACK OF MATTRESSES.
("THE PRINCESS AND THE PEA")

Fairy Tales & Other Folktales

What seven friends did Snow White have?

DWARFS

Mythology

Who hid inside the Trojan horse?

GREEK SOLDIERS

Mythology

What female monster had snakes growing from her head?

MEDUSA

Mythology

Who was transformed into a spider because she bragged about her fine weaving?

ARACHNE

Mythology

Who searched for a golden fleece?

JASON

Mythology

Who killed the monster Medusa?

PERSEUS

Mythology

What greedy king wished that everything he touched would turn to gold?

KING MIDAS

Mythology

Who holds the world on
his shoulders?

ATLAS

Mythology

What two brothers supposedly
founded Rome, Italy?

ROMULUS AND REMUS

Mythology

What lady was the cause of the
Trojan war?

HELEN

Mythology

Who was chief of the Norse gods?

ODIN

Mythology

Who were the creatures in Greek
mythology who were half man,
half horse?

CENTAURS

Mythology

Who was the much-loved
god of goodness and light
in Norse mythology?

BALDER

Mythology

In Norse mythology, who has a magic hammer?

THOR

Mythology

Where do Greek gods and goddesses live?

MOUNT OLYMPUS

Mythology

Where do Norse gods and goddesses live?

ASGARD

Mythology

What creature did Pandora manage to keep in the box?

HOPE

Mythology

Who died when he flew too close to the sun?

ICARUS

Mythology

What old couple were transformed into trees?

BAUCIS AND PHILEMON

Mythology

Who was the ruler of
Mount Olympus?

ZEUS (GREEK) OR
JUPITER (ROMAN)

Mythology

Who opened a box and let evil
enter the world?

PANDORA

Mythology

Who was the Greek god of
the sea?

POSEIDON
(ROMAN GOD—NEPTUNE)

Mythology

What son of Zeus was
extremely strong?

HERCULES

Mythology

What Greek god was a messenger
and had wings upon his feet?

HERMES
(ROMAN GOD—MERCURY)

Mythology

What mythological creature has
only one huge eye?

CYCLOPS